Meet the Dolphins

Written by
Jill Atkins

Andrew, Laura and Joe went to visit Gran.

"We are going to have fun looking into facts on dolphins," said Gran.

"I like dolphins," said Joe.

"Me too," said Laura.

"I bet I will get loads of facts," said Andrew.

Andrew and Laura looked in books. Joe looked on the internet. They spotted lots of interesting facts on dolphins.

Dolphins are not fish. They are mammals, like us!

Dolphins have dark skin. Now and then they have a pattern, or spots, as well.

They have a dorsal fin and a long tail.

It is usual for the mum to feed her new little dolphins on milk.

Dolphins have lungs, not gills. They can swim deep down but need to come up for air.

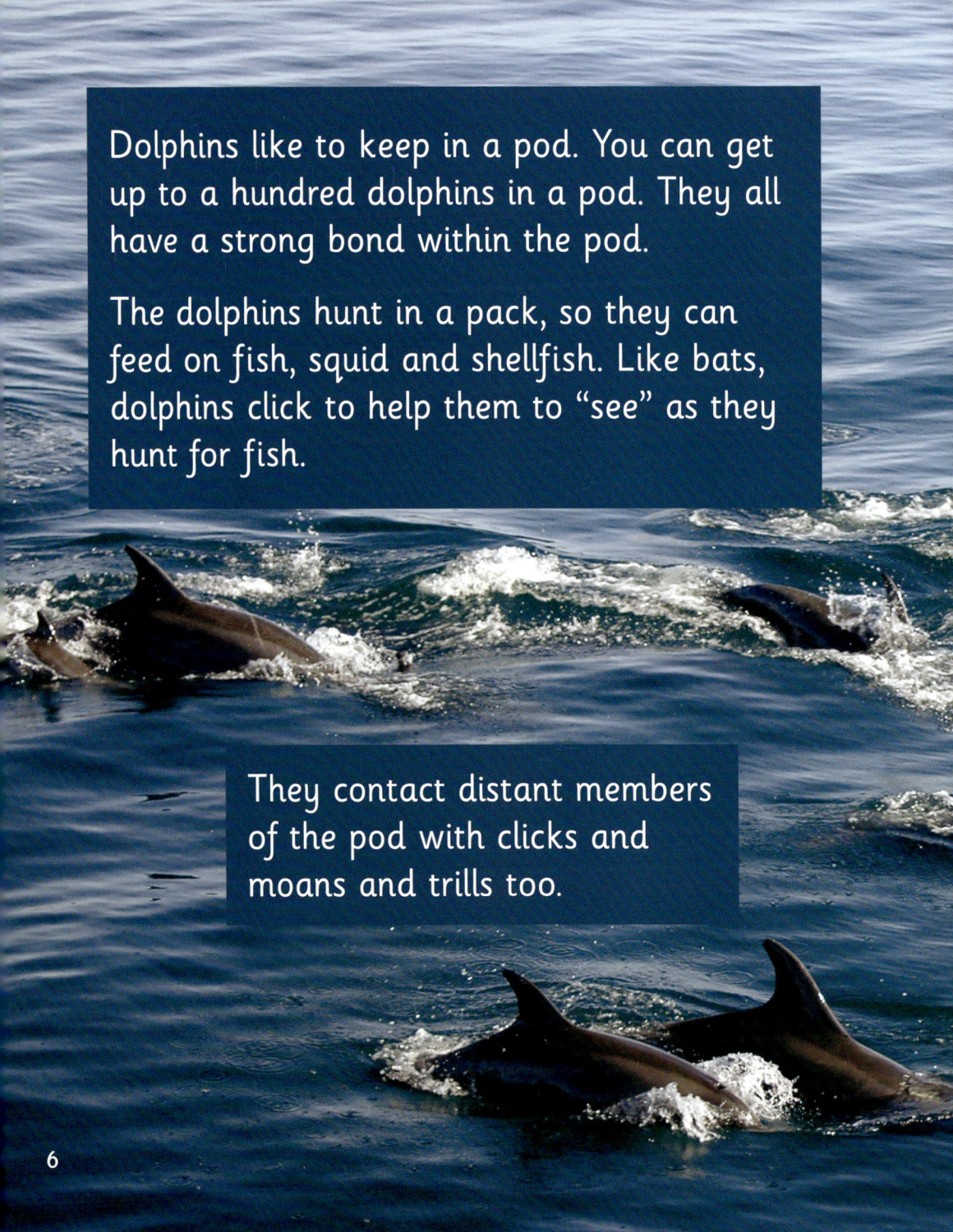

Dolphins like to keep in a pod. You can get up to a hundred dolphins in a pod. They all have a strong bond within the pod.

The dolphins hunt in a pack, so they can feed on fish, squid and shellfish. Like bats, dolphins click to help them to "see" as they hunt for fish.

They contact distant members of the pod with clicks and moans and trills too.

Some dolphins have fewer than one hundred teeth, but they do not chew the food.

Dolphins have thin skin, so they can get hurt.

If this happens, the dolphins in the pod will help.

They help the sick dolphins in the pod.

This is an orca. It is the biggest sort of dolphin.

This orca blew a jet as it popped up.

Little dolphins can be dinner for an orca.

Some sorts of dolphins inhabit rivers.

This is a river dolphin in Brazil.

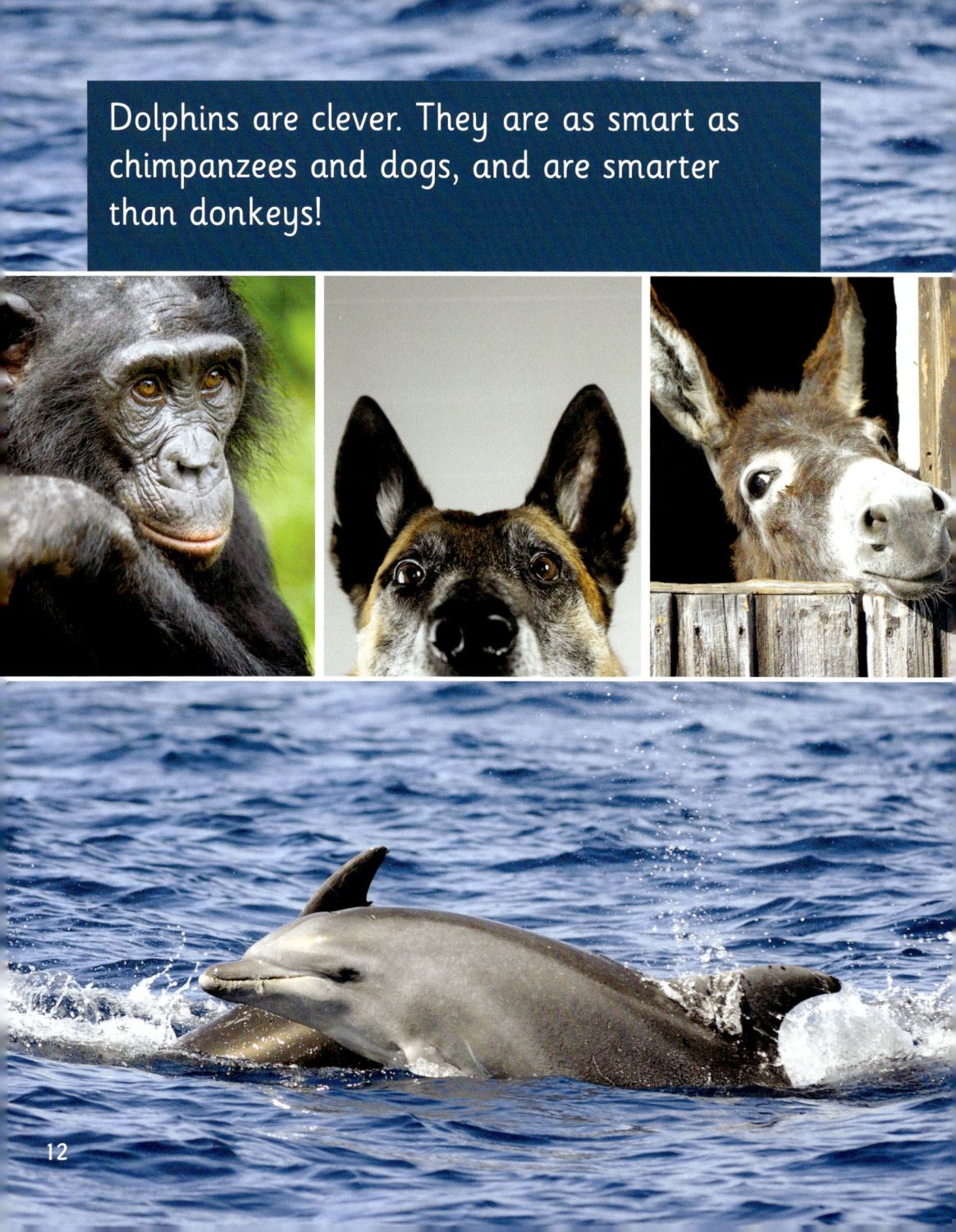

Dolphins are clever. They are as smart as chimpanzees and dogs, and are smarter than donkeys!

Dolphins like to have fun!

This dolphin can launch itself into the air then splash down again.

This dolphin can stand upright on its tail.

This dolphin flew in an arc.

It is an odd fact that dolphins can sleep as they swim. As they sleep, they rest just one part of the brain.

In pools, dolphins do stunts and tricks.

Some people like to swim with the dolphins. Some people like to look at the dolphins having fun.

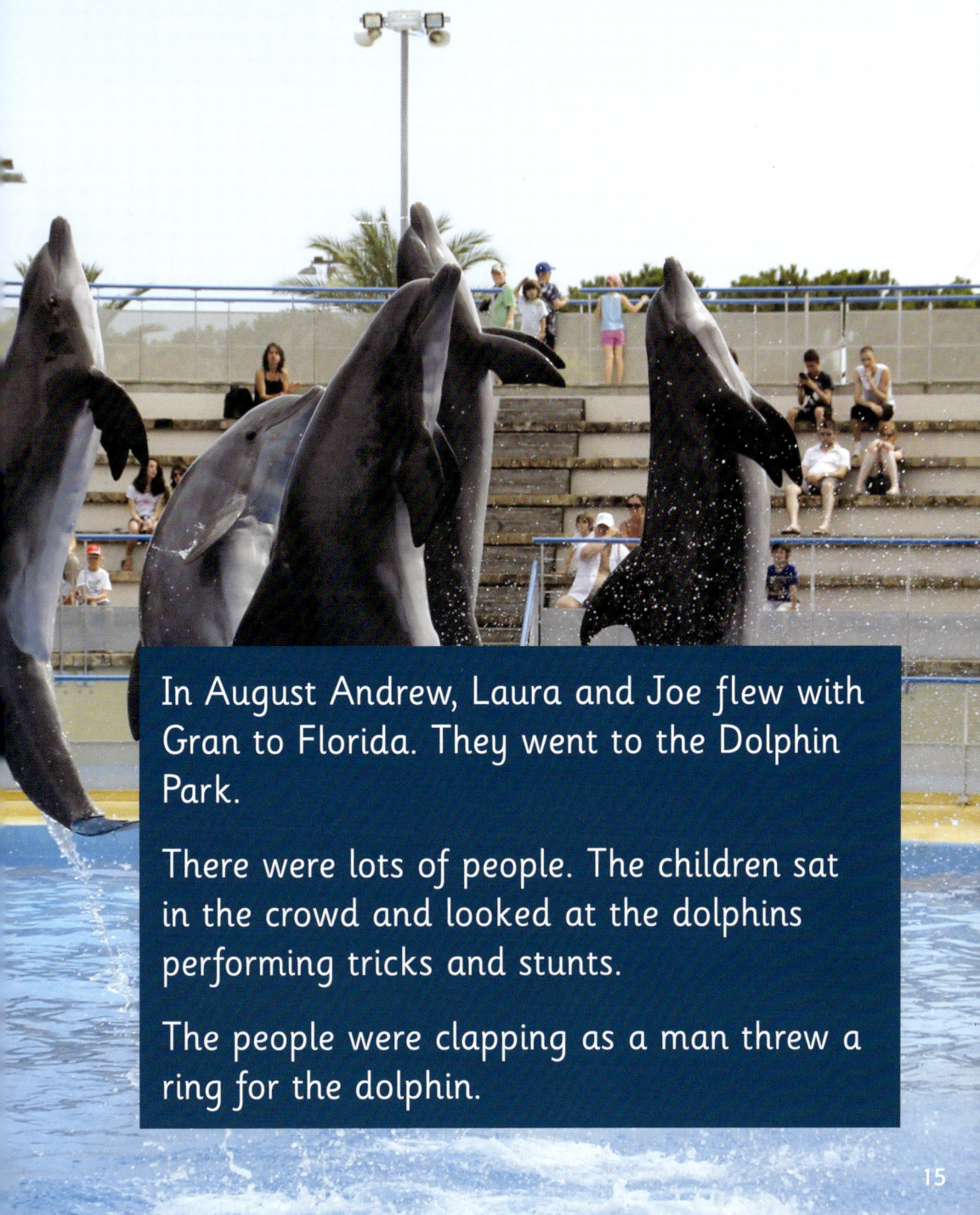

In August Andrew, Laura and Joe flew with Gran to Florida. They went to the Dolphin Park.

There were lots of people. The children sat in the crowd and looked at the dolphins performing tricks and stunts.

The people were clapping as a man threw a ring for the dolphin.

Dolphins are fantastic and clever!

But is it right to keep dolphins in a park just to entertain people? What do you think?